57

-9 JUL 2001

CW00519924

05. APR 02

A

27. JUN 02
03. AUG 02

29. MAY 03

13. SEP 04

15. DEC

346.41078

MARSH, D

A straightforward guide to bankruptcy, insolvency and the law

70002090464          Pbk

Please return/renew this item by the last date shown

Straightforward Publishing
www.Straightforwardco.co.uk

Straightforward Publishing
38 Cromwell Road
London E17 9JN

© Straightforward Publishing 2001

ISBN 1 899924 64 7

Printed by Bath Press Bath Somerset

Cover design by Straightforward Graphics.

# CONTENTS

Introduction

1. The Law  7
   Insolvency Acts
   The courts
   Key points

2. Individual Bankruptcy  11
   The statutory demand
   Compliance with the demand
   Key points

3. The Bankruptcy Petition  17
   Issue of petition
   Service of petition
   Hearing the petition
   Substitution
   Dismissal and withdrawal
   Key points

4. The Hearing  27
   The hearing
   Statement of affairs
   Key points

5. Trustees and Creditors  33
   Appointment of trustees and a creditors committee
   Types of creditor
   key points

6. General Points  37
   Interest
   Dividends
   Discharge from bankruptcy
   Offences whilst bankrupt
   Criminal action
   Rights of the bankrupt and powers of the trustee
   Key points

# 7. Individual Voluntary Arrangements 43
Individual voluntary arrangements
Key points

# 8. Insolvent partnerships 47
Winding up a partnership
Partners own petition for a bankruptcy order
Key points

# 9. Insolvent Estates 51
The Administration of Insolvent Estates Act 1986
Key points

# 10. Compulsory Liquidation 55
Compulsory liquidation
Preparing and serving the demand
Creditors petitions
The hearing of the petition
Before and after the company winding up
Appointment of a provisional liquidator
Public examination
Appointing a liquidator
Key points

# 11. Creditors Voluntary Liquidation 65
Members voluntary liquidation
Creditors voluntary liquidation
Key points

# 12. All Liquidations 67
The powers of the liquidator
Mutual credit and sell off
Adjustment of prior transactions
Debts and dividends
Provable debts
Proofs of debts
Interest
V.A.T
Dividends
Key points

## 13. Receiverships  77
Nature of receivership
Priority of debts in receivership
Powers of a receiver
Duties of a receiver
Statement of affairs
V.A.T
Key points

## 14. Company voluntary Arrangements  81
Nature of a company voluntary arrangement
Meetings of shareholders and creditors
Key points

## 15. Administration  85
Nature of administration
Application for an administration order
Powers of the administrator
Power to deal with charged property
Summoning creditors meetings
Discharge or variation of the administration order
Investigation by the administrator
V.A.T
Key points

Glossary of terms  91
Appendix 1: Courts dealing with bankruptcy  93
Index  102

# INTRODUCTION

This Second Edition of *A Straightforward Guide to Bankruptcy, Insolvency and the Law* is a comprehensive overview of the processes involved in bankruptcy and insolvency, which builds on the first edition by updating relevant areas of law and practice throughout the text. The book deals with individuals, partnerships and companies and outlines the law underpinning each area. The steps in the procedure are clearly outlined, from the original serving of notice to gaining a bankruptcy order.

Whilst the approach adopted is a functional one, it is realised that the whole process of bankruptcy is unpleasant, undermining a persons dignity and sometimes stigmatising that person. Certainly, bankruptcy affects significantly a person's position in relation to further business.

In addition, those who attempt to recover debts from a company that is becoming insolvent often lose out, sometimes a great deal of money.

This book does not attempt to address those issues, although the author recognises them. It is, above all, a step by step guide that will clearly demonstrate the whole area of insolvency and bankruptcy. The book will be suitable for a whole range of people, from the person in the street, the student, and also the advisor.

Finally, if you are about to take the first steps on the road to bankruptcy, or making a person bankrupt, or a company insolvent, take advice at the outset. Although the basic steps are, in principle, straightforward, the whole process can become very complex indeed.

David Marsh,
London March 2001.

# 1
# THE LAW

The Insolvency Act of 1986, which came into effect on the 29th of December 1986, is the Act regulating all matters to do with Bankruptcy.

There are also Statutory Instruments-The Insolvency Rules 1986, The Insolvent Partnerships Order 1986, Administration of Insolvent Estates of Deceased Persons Order 1986, Insolvency Practitioner Regulations 1986, Insolvency Proceedings (monetary limits) Order 1986, Insolvency Fees Order 1986, Co-operation of Insolvency Court (Designation of relevant countries and Territories Order) 1986, which regulate bankruptcy.

The parts of the Act relating to companies applies not only to England and Wales but also to Scotland. All insolvencies commenced before December 29th 1986 continue to be subject to the Bankruptcy Act 1914 or the Companies Act 1985, as the case may be.

There are transitional provisions in the Act such as power for the Secretary of State to appoint trustees or liquidators to old Act cases, automatic discharge from bankruptcy of all old Act Bankrupts on 29th December 1989 and power for the trustee or liquidator to agree costs (instead of taxation).

To take the first steps towards making an individual bankrupt, it is necessary to have the grounds to do so and also to choose the right court to which to make an application to petition.

A statutory demand is often prepared and served, as non-compliance with such a demand is one of the grounds for petitioning for bankruptcy.

## The courts

The **High Court** has jurisdiction in bankruptcy proceedings if any one of the following criteria applies:

The debtor has resided or carried on business within the London insolvency district for the greater part of the last six months or for a longer period than in any other insolvency district;

The person is not resident in England or Wales;

His residence or place of business is unknown to the petitioner;

The petition is presented by a government department based on an unsatisfied execution or a statutory demand in which it is stated that if a bankruptcy petition was necessary, it would be presented in the high court.

## The County Court

The county Court has jurisdiction over all other cases. A bankruptcy petition must be presented in the county court for the insolvency district in which the debtor has lived or carried on business for the longest period in the last six months (before petition). If residence and business areas are separate, it is the business address that determines the court. If business is carried on in more than one area it is the principal place of business that determines. If the debtor is already the subject of an individual voluntary arrangement (IVA) then the court dealing with the IVA must deal with the bankruptcy.

Now read the key points from Chapter One overleaf.

## KEY POINTS FROM CHAPTER ONE

- The Insolvency Act of 1986 regulates all matters connected with bankruptcy. All of the necessary standard forms are contained within this Act.

- The High Court and the county court deal with bankruptcy, subject to certain criteria mentioned in this chapter.

# 2
# INDIVIDUAL BANKRUPTCY

## MAKING THE DEMAND

### The statutory demand

The statutory demand referred to earlier is a document prepared by the creditor in the prescribed form requiring the debtor to pay the debt referred to in the demand or to make an arrangement to pay or provide security to pay the debt within three weeks after the demand is served.

There are three forms of statutory demand set out in (schedule four) to the rules:

form 6.1-demand for a debt presently due but not based on a judgement.

form 6.2-demand for a debt presently due based on a judgement or order of the court.

form 6.3-demand for a debt due at a future time.

When completing the form, the full name of the debtor should be given, along with the full name and address of the creditor. Only one debt can be included as the debt on the form. The amount of the debt must be stated and interest if claimed.

A statutory demand can only be made for an unsecured debt and if the creditor holds any security he must specify what it is and put a value on it so that the amount of unsecured portion of his debt can be identified.

it so that the amount of unsecured portion of his debt can be identified. The demand must be signed by the creditor himself or someone authorised on his behalf, such as a solicitor. A solicitors firm signing on behalf of an individual must ensure that the demand is signed by an individual solicitor and not by the firm as a whole.

On page 2 of the demand, the court to which the debtor can apply to have the demand set aside must be given. This will either be the High Court (if the debtor resides or carries on business in the area of London Insolvency District) or one of the County Courts specified in the Appendix).

The prescribed period for compliance with the demand is 21 days but if the demand has been served abroad, different time limits apply and must be inserted in the demand in accordance with the extra jurisdiction tables to be found in the Supreme Court Practice. If the debt is payable at a future time, form 6.3 must be used instead and the creditor must state why he believes the debtor has no reasonable prospects of paying the debt when it falls due.

The demand must be served personally, and the creditor must bring the demand, if possible, to the debtors attention. If personal service is not possible, then postal service will suffice, as long as proof of service can be demonstrated and is seen as justified. If service by advertisement is used (this can only apply if the creditor has obtained a judgement against the debtor) time runs from the date of the first advertisement.

An affidavit of service of the demand is required. There are prescribed forms of affidavit:

* form 6.11- personal service
* form 6.12- substituted service

Form 6.11 is the more commonly required. The affidavit of service must exhibit the demand, any acknowledgement in writing from the debtor and a copy of the newspaper advertisement (where applicable).

## Compliance with the demand

If the debtor does not comply with the demand within three weeks the debtor is deemed as unable to comply with the demand. The day the demand was served and the day the petition was presented are ignored for the purpose of calculating if the correct time has been allowed. Similar rules apply for calculating the period of 18 days within which the debtor must apply to the court for the demand to be set aside if he so wishes. Service after 4pm on a business day or service on a weekend or bank holiday is deemed to have taken place on the next business day. If the creditor can show that there is a serious possibility of the debtors property being diminished in value in the three week period after service of a demand, a petition can be presented sooner (though not until after the statutory demand has been served) but a bankruptcy order cannot be made until after the three week period has elapsed.

Quite often, if there is a mistake in service or content of demands, as with other court notices, the court might set them aside if a debtor has been prejudiced. However, mistakes in demand have to be considerable for a court to do this. Even if the debt has been overstated, so long as the debt exceeds £750 in any case, then the demand will not be set aside.

The application by a debtor to set aside a demand must be made within 18 days after the service of the demand. The court has power to extend the time for applying and will usually grant leave for a late application if any reason for the delay is given. The application for an extension of time is made to the High Court or circuit judge (not registrar or district judge). The fee payable is set down in the list of current court costs which can be obtained from the courts.

An affidavit in support of an application is required to set aside a demand stating when the demand was received and the grounds of the application. A copy of the demand must be exhibited. Four copies of the application and the affidavit must be lodged together with the current court fee. The application will then be heard by the registrar or the district judge. Examples of the reasons for asking for a demand to be set aside are:

* the debt is disputed in whole or part (and there is not at least £750 admitted).

* the debt is not payable now.

* the debtor is prepared to secure or compound for the debt to the creditors satisfaction in the creditors stated way.

* the debt is secured.

* the debtor has a counterclaim or set off equal to or exceeding the claim.

* execution of the judgement has been stayed.

* the demand does not comply with the rules.

The application must be made in the appropriate court. The application automatically causes the time for compliance with the demand to cease to run. If the registrar or the district judge reading the papers is satisfied that the application is without merit, he may dismiss it without a hearing or notice to the creditor. If he is satisfied that the application has some merit, a hearing date will be fixed and notice will be given to the creditor or his solicitor.

At the hearing, if the court is satisfied that the debtor has a case, the demand will be set aside and the creditor is liable to have the costs of the application awarded against him. If the demand is not set aside, the court may make an order authorising the creditor to present a bankruptcy petition at a specified time.

Now read the key points from Chapter Two overleaf.

## KEY POINTS FROM CHAPTER TWO

- When making an individual bankrupt, it is necessary to serve a statutory demand on that person.

- A Statutory demand can only be made for an unsecured debt. The prescribed period for compliance is 21 days and it must be served personally. If this is not possible then postal service will suffice as long as proof of service can be demonstrated.

- The application by a debtor to set aside a demand must be made within 18 days after service of this demand.

# 3
# THE BANKRUPTCY PETITION

For a bankruptcy petition to be presented to the court, three conditions must be satisfied:

* the debtor must be domiciled or personally resident or carry on business in England and Wales on the day on which the petition is presented or at any time in the previous three years.

* the debt owed by the debtor (or the total of the debts owed to the petitioners if there are more than two of them) must be above the minimum level of £750 and be a liquidated sum payable immediately or at some certain future time.

* the debtor must be unable to pay the debt or have no reasonable prospect of being unable to pay. This requirement has been satisfied if the debtor has been served with a statutory demand and has failed to comply with it nor had it set aside or an execution or other process issued against him in respect of that debt has been returned unsatisfied in whole or in part.

There are four prescribed forms of petition set out in the rules:

* form 6.7-on failure to comply with a statutory demand, debt payable immediately.

* form 6.8-on failure to comply with a statutory demand, debt payable at a future date.

* form 6.9-where execution returns unsatisfied.

* form 6.10-on default in connection with IVA.

If two or more creditors jointly petition, all their details must be set out. Anyone who can sue the debtor for the debt is classed as a creditor of the debtor for the purposes of the petition. Secured creditors must value their security and can only petition for the unsecured part of their debt or risk forfeiting their security.

The following information relating to the debtor must be given:

* name, address, place of residence and occupation.

* the names in which that person carried on business, if other than his true name and if alone or with others.

* the nature and address of his business.

* Any previous names used by the debtor at the time the debt was incurred.

* his residential or business address at the time the debt was incurred.

If the creditor knows that the debtor has used any other name, this must be stated in the petition. The petition must state:

*the amount, the consideration for it and the fact that it is still owing if interest has been included how it has been calculated and the grounds for claiming it.

* that the debt is for a liquidated sum payable immediately and the debtor is unable to pay it or that the debt is payable at a certain future time and the debtor appears to have no reasonable prospect of being able to pay and, in either case, the debt is unsecured.

If the petition is based upon a statutory demand, only the debt claimed in the demand can be included and interest accrued since the demand was served cannot be included. If the petition is based upon an unsatisfied execution, full particulars of the issuing court and the sheriffs or bailiffs return must be given.

If the petition is based upon non compliance with statutory demand, care must be taken to recite correctly the details of service and in particular whether the service was effected before or after 4pm on business days or before or after 12 noon on Saturdays. It is no longer necessary to search to see if monies have been paid into the county court in satisfaction of any judgement debt obtained in that court.

It is still desirable to search for prior bankruptcy petitions even though there is no requirement to do so. The court tends to carry out such a search itself, but effort and cost can be saved by ascertaining before a further petition is issued that there is already one pending.

A bankruptcy petition must be verified by an affidavit. If the petition is based on failure to comply with a statutory demand and more than four months have elapsed since the demand was served, the reasons for the delay must be given in the affidavit. If no adequate explanation is given, the petition may be dismissed under section 266 (3) but the court cannot refuse to allow the petition to be issued. The affidavit verifying the petition must exhibit a copy of the petition.

## Issue of petition

On issue the following are required:

* the petition together with two copies (and a further copy if voluntary arrangement is in force)

* if the petition is based upon failure to comply with a statutory demand, the affidavit of service of the demand.

* an affidavit verifying the petition.

* a receipt for the deposit payable to the  Official Receiver-costs can be obtained from  the local court.

* the fee-current court costs.

All copies of the petition are sealed by the court and, save for one, handed back to the petitioner. The petition is endorsed by the court with details of the time, date and place of the hearing.

**Service of the petition**

A sealed copy of the petition must be served personally on the debtor by a court bailiff, the petitioning creditor or his solicitor, or someone instructed on their behalf. If the service is effected after 4pm on a business day or after 12 noon on a Saturday, service is deemed to have been effected on the next business day. If a voluntary arrangement is in force, the supervisor must be served as well as the debtor unless it is the supervisor who is petitioning.

An affidavit of service of the petition is required which must exhibit a sealed copy of the petition and, when substituted service has been ordered, a copy of that order. The affidavit of service must be filed in court immediately after service. The form of affidavit of service is form 6.17. If substituted service has been used, because of non co-operation of debtor, then form 6.18 is used. Where two or more petitions have been presented against the same debtor, the court can order the consolidation of the proceedings as it sees fit.

**Hearing the petition**

The petition cannot be heard until at least 14 days have elapsed since it was served unless the court is satisfied that an expedited hearing is warranted, the debtor is about to abscond or the debtor consents to an early hearing. If the debtor wishes to oppose the petition he must give notice to the petitioning creditor and file at court a notice specifying the grounds of his objection. A petition may be amended at any time with leave of the court.

Any creditor who intends to appear on the hearing of the petition must give notice to the petitioning creditor. The notice must state the amount of his debt and whether he intends to support or oppose the petition. The notice is form 6.20 in schedule 4 to the Act. The petitioning creditor must prepare a list of the creditors, if any, who have given notice of intention to appear or state on such a list that there are no creditors who have given notice of intention to appear. The list is prescribed form 6.21. The list is handed to the court clerk before the commencement of the hearing. If the petitioning creditor fails to appear on the hearing, the petition may be dismissed and no further petitions against the same debtor would be allowed, without leave of the court. It is not necessary for the petitioning creditor himself to appear at the hearing if he is represented by solicitors.

The courts are unwilling to adjourn a petition more than once since it must not be allowed to hang over the debtors head indefinitely. If, however, insufficient time has elapsed since the debtor was served with the petition, the hearing must be adjourned. If there is an adjournment, the petitioning creditor must inform all those creditors who have given notice of intention to appear and also inform the debtor. The order adjourning the petition is prepared by the court and the notice of adjournment is prepared by the petitioning creditor.

## Substitution

If the petitioning creditors debt has been paid, the court may order that another creditor be substituted as petitioning creditor provided that the creditor has given notice of his intention to appear on the hearing and prosecute his petition.

As an alternative to seeking substitution as petitioning creditor, if a creditor has given notice of his intention to appear on the hearing he may apply to the court for an order giving him control of the proceedings in place of the petitioning creditor.

## Dismissal and withdrawal

A petition cannot be withdrawn except at the hearing and the court will dismiss a petition or give leave for it to be withdrawn only if the petitioning creditor files at court an affidavit setting out why he wants the petition dismissed or withdrawn. The affidavit must include details of any payments made by the debtor or arrangements for the securing or compounding of the debt together with details of where the monies came from that were used to pay or secure or compound the debt.

On an application for leave to withdraw the petition or for dismissal of the petition, it is the practice of the court to adjourn the petition to a new hearing date so as to enable any other creditor to make an application to be substituted as petitioning creditor. The form of dismissal of a petition is form 6.22.

On hearing of the petition, the petitioning creditor must satisfy the court that the debt is still owing. A certificate in the following form, signed by the person representing the petitioning creditor will suffice:

I certify that I have (my firm has) made enquiries of the petitioning creditor within the last business day prior to the hearing/adjourned hearing and to the best of my knowledge and belief the debt(s) on which the petition is founded is still due and owing and has not been paid or secured or compounded for.

Signed

Dated

A fresh certificate is required on each adjourned hearing.

Now read the key points from Chapter Three overleaf.

## KEY POINTS FROM CHAPTER THREE

- For a bankruptcy petition to be presented to the court, three conditions must be satisfied: The debtor must be domiciled or personally resident or carry on business in England and Wales on the day on which the petition is presented or at any time in the previous three years: the debt owed by the debtor (or the total of the debts owed to the petitioners if there are more than two of them) must be above the minimum level of £750 and be a liquidated sum payable immediately or at some certain future time: the debtor must be unable to pay the debt or have no reasonable prospect of being able to pay.

- There are four prescribed forms of petition set out in the rules.

- If two or more creditors jointly petition, all their details must be set out. Anyone can sue the debtor for the debt is classed as a creditor of the debtor for the purpose of the petition.

- If the petition is based upon a statutory demand, only the debt claimed in the demand can be included and interest accrued since the demand was served cannot be included.

- A bankruptcy petition must be verified by an affidavit. If the petition is based on failure to comply with a statutory demand and more than four months have elapsed since the demand was served, the reasons for the delay must be given in the affidavit.

- A sealed copy of the petition must be served personally on the debtor by a court bailiff.

- The petition cannot be heard until at least 14 days have elapsed since it was served unless the court is satisfied that an expedited hearing is warranted, the debtor is about to abscond or the debtor consents to an early hearing.

# 4
# THE HEARING

## The hearing

For a bankruptcy order to be made, the court must be satisfied that the debt in respect of which the petition was presented has neither been paid or, if the debt is due at a future time, the debtor has no reasonable prospect of being able to meet the debt.

The court will dismiss the petition if it is satisfied that the debtor can meet his debts. If it is satisfied that the facts in the petition are true, it may make a bankruptcy order. It is discretionary.

A debtor may present his own bankruptcy petition on the grounds that he cannot meet debts. Any such petition must be accompanied by a prescribed form that details a statement of the debtors affairs. Copies of the prescribed form can be obtained from the court or the official receiver. When issuing a debtors petition three copies should be presented along with two copies of statement of affairs, a receipt for the deposit-currently £135 and the current court fee.

One copy of the petition is endorsed and returned to the debtor with a hearing date. The courts forward the remaining copies to the official receiver. The court may make a bankruptcy order on the hearing. If the liabilities are less than the current small bankruptcies level of £20,000, the court may issue a certificate for the summary administration of the estate. Alternatively, an insolvency practitioner may be appointed to prepare a report under s273. If the debts are less than the small bankruptcies level, and the assets are above the minimum level, currently £2,000, then the court must not make a bankruptcy order but should instead appoint an insolvency practitioner to prepare a report under section 273. Alternatively, an insolvency practitioner can be appointed to prepare a report.

The insolvency practitioner should then make a report to the court on whether or not the debtor is willing to enter into a voluntary arrangement and on whether a meeting of the creditors should be arranged. If a voluntary arrangement is entered into by the debtor then the court can make an interim bankruptcy order so as to facilitate the implementation of this arrangement.

The court draws up the bankruptcy order and serves copies on all parties. The official receiver will notify the chief land registrar and advertise in the London Gazette and the local papers. The court can also issue a certificate of summary administration. The effect of the certificate being issued is that there is no obligation on the official receiver to investigate the debtors conduct and the debtor can expect an automatic discharge at the end of two years rather than three.

If a person is made bankrupt, once the petition has been presented, any court may stay any action or other legal process against the debtor or his property. The granting of such a stay is discretionary. Once a bankruptcy order has been made, a creditor has no remedy against the person or property of the bankrupt and may not commence any action against him without leave of the court. A secured creditor is not affected by these provisions and can enforce his security though he cannot take any action in connection with any unsecured debts.

If it is necessary to protect the debtors property prior to the bankruptcy hearing, the court can, on application of debtor or creditor, appoint the official receiver as interim receiver. If an insolvency practitioner has been appointed (see above) that person can be appointed as interim receiver.

Any court having jurisdiction in bankruptcy may review, rescind or dispose of any order made by it. If the proceedings have been transferred from one court to another after the making of the bankruptcy order, the transferee court can exercise such powers. The court can annul a bankruptcy order if it considers it wrongly made or that all debts have been paid since the making of the order.

## Statement of affairs

Where a bankruptcy order is made, the bankrupt is obliged to submit a statement of affairs. In the case of a debtors own petition, the statement of affairs will have been included with the papers lodged with the court. The statement must be submitted to the Official Receiver within 21 days of making the bankruptcy order. The statement must contain full particulars of creditors and other liabilities and assets. The Official Receiver is obliged to give the bankrupt copies of this form.

If the bankrupt cannot prepare a statement of affairs, the official receiver can appoint someone to do this at the bankrupts expense. The official receiver can require the bankrupt to furnish three years accounts prior to bankruptcy. The court can order accounts for a longer period to be submitted and also request further information.

There is no automatic public examination of a bankrupt, as used to be the practice. If an official receiver wishes to publicly examine a bankrupt then they must make application to the court. A creditor can also make such a request if he is owed more than 50% of total debts by the debtor. If the bankrupt fails to attend a public examination ordered by the court he will be guilty of contempt of court. However, if the bankrupt wishes to be examined in some other way then he can make an application to the court.

At the public examination, the official receiver, the trustee and any creditor can ask questions. Such an ordeal is often very stressful for the bankrupt. A solicitor can represent the bankrupt. There is no entitlement to refuse to answer questions although if criminal proceedings have commenced against the bankrupt and the questioning may prejudice such proceedings then questioning can be adjourned.

Now read the key points from Chapter Four Overleaf.

## KEY POINTS FROM CHAPTER FOUR

- A debtor may present his own bankruptcy petition on the grounds that he cannot meet debts. If the liabilities are less than the court small bankruptcies level of £20,000, the court may issue a certificate for the summary administration of the estate.

- If a person is made bankrupt, once a petition is presented, any court may stay any action or other legal process against the debtor or his family.

- If it is necessary to protect the debtors property prior to the bankruptcy hearing, the court can appoint the Official Receiver as an interim receiver.

- Where a bankruptcy order is made, the bankrupt is obliged to submit a statement of affairs outlining his circumstances.

# 5
# TRUSTEES AND CREDITORS

## Appointment of trustees and a creditors committee

The trustee can be appointed by a general meeting of the creditors (except where there is in force a certificate of summary administration), by the court (where a bankruptcy follows on a voluntary arrangement), or by the Secretary of State (where the creditors have failed to appoint a trustee and the Official Receiver considers one necessary). No person can be appointed trustee unless he is an authorised insolvency practitioner. Two or more trustees can be appointed to act jointly.

The official receiver must decide within 12 weeks after the making of the bankruptcy order whether or not to summon a meeting of creditors for the purpose of choosing someone to be a trustee. If such a meeting is called, this must be held not more than four months from the date of the bankruptcy order and 21 days notice must be given to all creditors. Notice must also be given by inserting an advertisement in a local paper and the London Gazette. If the official receiver receives a notice from a creditor supported by at least 25% in value of all other creditors, he must call a meeting.

Any notice of a meeting to creditors must include a form of proxy to enable creditors who cannot attend to forward someone on their behalf.

It is important to be familiar with the rules governing any creditors meetings. At the initial meeting, the official receiver will chair and the trustee will chair subsequent meetings. Any resolutions are deemed to trustee will chair subsequent meetings. Any resolutions are deemed to be passed on a majority in value of the creditors present personally or by proxy who vote in favour of it. A quorum must be present which consists of at least one creditor in person or in proxy. If the meeting has to be adjourned, it must not be adjourned for longer than 21 days.

The primary purpose of the first meeting of creditors is to appoint a trustee. No person can be appointed as a trustee unless he is a qualified insolvency practitioner. During any vacancy of the post of trustee, such as death of a trustee, the official receiver becomes trustee. A trustee other than the official receiver can be removed by a vote of the creditors committee. Proper notice of such a meeting has to be given. the court may also remove a trustee on application of an interested person and the secretary of State may remove a trustee.

**Types of Creditor**

There are four classes of creditor-secured, preferential, unsecured and deferred. A secured creditor, although being in a strong position on the basis of having his debts secured, is not given any special priority when it comes to repayment, but can rely on security. Preferential debts are defined in section 386 and schedule 6 to the Act. They consist primarily of taxes such as VAT, PAYE and social security contributions. Amounts due to employees for wages for the four months prior to the making of the bankruptcy order but not exceeding £800 for each employee are also preferential together with any arrears of holiday pay. Unsecured creditors are the ordinary debts of the bankrupt that are neither secured or preferential. Deferred debts are those owed by the bankrupt to his spouse. These debts rank after the preferential and ordinary unsecured creditors.

Every person claiming to be a creditor must submit his claim in writing to the official receiver or trustee-this is called proving his debt. A proof of debt is in prescribed form that is sent out by the official receiver. Proof of debt must contain details of the creditors name and address, the amount owing, the date of the bankruptcy order, whether interest and VAT is included, whether any part of the debt is preferential, how the debt was incurred and particulars of any security and its value.

There is no time limit for submission of proofs of debt but a creditor who has not proved his debt cannot benefit from any distribution of the bankrupts assets. Before declaring a dividend, the trustee must give notice of his intention to do so to all creditors of whom he is aware and who have not proved their debts. The notice must specify the last date for proving, which must not be less than 21 days after the date of the notice.

## KEY POINTS FROM CHAPTER FIVE

- The trustees can be appointed by a general meeting of creditors or by the court or by the Secretary of State. The person appointed must be an authorised Insolvency Practitioner.

- The Official Receiver must decide within 12 months after the making of the bankruptcy order whether or not to summon a meeting of creditors for the purpose of appointing a trustee.

- There are four classes of creditor-secured, preferential, unsecured and deferred.

- Every person claiming to be a creditor must submit a claim in writing to the Official Receiver to prove his debt.

# 6
# GENERAL POINTS

## Interest

When a bankrupts debt bears interest, either contractual or statutory, the proof of debt can include interest up to the date of the bankruptcy order. If the debt does not include the right to interest, interest can still be claimed at the judgement rate up to the date of the bankruptcy order, subject to certain qualifications, such as whether the debt arose by virtue of a written instrument and in respect of a debt payable at a certain time after notice of intention to claim interest has been given.

## Dividends

A trustee must give notice of his intention to pay a dividend to all creditors who have proven their debts. The notice must include details of the amounts realised from the sale of their assets, payments made by the trustees in the administration of the estate, the total amount distributed, the rate of dividend and whether any further dividends are to be expected. The trustee must not, except with the leave of the court, proceed to declare a dividend where there is a pending application to vary a decision of the trustee on a proof of debt. If the trustee is unable to declare any or further dividend, he must give notice to this effect to creditors.

## Discharge from bankruptcy

For those people who have not been made bankrupt within the last 15 years or who have not been made criminally bankrupt, an automatic discharge from bankruptcy is usually made after three years. Where a discharge from bankruptcy is usually made after three years. Where a certificate of summary administration is in force, the period is two years. The courts however, have to be satisfied that the bankrupt has satisfied his obligations under the Insolvency Act.

If the Official Receiver wants the right to automatic discharge to be suspended he should apply to court. The bankrupt can contest this, also in court. If a person has been bankrupt in the previous fifteen years, or criminally bankrupt, he has to apply to the court for discharge. This can only be done five years after the granting of the original bankruptcy order.

Whenever a bankrupt person is discharged the court must, at the request of the bankrupt, issue a certificate of discharge. The bankrupt can also require the Secretary of State to advertise his discharge in the London Gazette.

**Offences whilst bankrupt**

Although bankruptcy does not constitute a crime, there are offences set out in the Insolvency Act for which a Bankrupt can be prosecuted. For example, it is an offence to be a company director whilst an un-discharged bankrupt. Concealment of property is an offence, false statements, fraudulent disposal of property and absconding whilst bankrupt, gambling or obtaining credit without disclosing bankruptcy, are all offences and the bankrupt can be prosecuted under various sections of the Insolvency Act.

**Criminal action**

The Criminal Justice Act 1988 contains provisions relating to criminal bankruptcy. If a person has been made bankrupt as a result of a criminal bankruptcy order there is no automatic right to discharge. This is at the discretion of the courts and five years must elapse before application.

Where a person has been convicted of an offence by the Crown Court or the magistrates court and it appears that the loss or damage has been suffered by one or more persons of at least £10,000 the court may make a confiscation order. The court can make a restraint order to prevent the accused from disposing of property prior to the conclusion of the proceedings.

## Rights of the bankrupt and powers of a trustee

Any property acquired by the bankrupt after a bankruptcy order has been made against him does not automatically become part of the estate to be disposed of by a trustee. The trustee may, however, claim that property for the benefit of that estate by giving notice within 42 days of first learning about the property.

The trustee has no right to claim the tools and personal effects of the bankrupt. A bankrupt is authorised to continue in business providing that he informs everyone from whom he try's to obtain credit of more than £250 that he is a bankrupt. The bankrupt person is entitled to retain such tools, books, vehicles and other items and equipment as are necessary for his use personally by him in his employment, business or vocation but he should inform the trustee not less than once every six months of information relating to any business carried out by him.

The trustee can ask the court for an order requiring the bankrupt to pay some of his income into the bankrupts estate. The court must not require the bankrupt to make any payments that might affect the well being of him and his family.

Where the bankrupt has a spouse and the trustee wishes to obtain an order for sale of the property so as to realise the bankrupts interest in that property, he must make application under the Matrimonial Homes Act 1983, s1, or the Law of Property Act 1925, s30 depending on whether the property is in the sole name of the bankrupt or joint names. In deciding whether or not to allow the trustee to insist on the sale of the property, the court will take into account the interest of the creditors, the conduct of the spouse so far as contributing to the bankruptcy, the needs and financial resources of the spouses and children and all the circumstances of the case except the needs of the husband.

If the trustees application is made after one year of the commencement of the bankruptcy, it will be presumed that the interest of the spouse outweighs all other interests. If the application is made after one year, then the presumption is the other way round. if the bankrupt has no spouse or children living with him, he has no right to remain living in the property.

The trustee in bankruptcy is in no better position than the bankrupts spouse and will be subject to those authorities on the determination of each spouses interest in the matrimonial home. If for any reason the trustee has been unable to realise his interest in the home, he cannot conclude his administration without first considering whether it is appropriate to impose a charge on the bankrupts property. The trustee may apply to the court for an order imposing a charge order on the property for the benefit of the estate. The charge would be for an equivalent of the deficiency in the estate.

Now read the key points from chapter six.

KEY POINTS FROM CHAPTER SIX

- Where a bankrupt debt bears interest, either contractual or statutory, the proof of debt can include interest up to the date of the bankruptcy order.

- A trustee must give notice of his intent to pay a dividend to all creditors who have proven their debts.

- An automatic discharge from bankruptcy is usually made after three years.

- It is an offence to be a company director whilst an undischarged bankrupt.

- If a person has been made bankrupt as a result of a criminal bankruptcy there is no automatic right of discharge.

- A bankrupt can keep tools and personal effects and can continue in business providing that he informs everyone from whom he try's to obtain credit of more than £250 that he is bankrupt.

41

# 7
# INDIVIDUAL VOLUNTARY ARRANGEMENTS

## Individual Voluntary arrangements

An individual voluntary arrangement (IVA) is an arrangement between an individual debtor and his creditors whereby the creditors agree either to accept something less than 100 pence in the pound on their debts in full and final settlement or agree to some deferment of the time for payment of their debts. An IVA is essentially a private matter between the debtor and his creditors with the involvement of a nominee/supervisor acting in a similar way as a trustee in bankruptcy. While an IVA is being proposed, protection from the court is obtained for the debtor from his creditors.

Only an individual debtor can make a proposal for an IVA-joint debtors such as partners cannot though they can enter into arrangements individually. The Insolvency Act 1986 sets out the details that must be contained in the proposal. These include a short explanation as to why the debtor thinks an IVA is desirable and why the creditors may be expected to agree to it, details of all assets and liabilities and what the cost of the IVA is likely to be.

Whether or not the debtor needs protection from his creditors whilst the proposals are being considered, he must apply to the court for an interim order. As soon as the application for an IVA has been lodged, application can be made ex parte for an order staying all actions against interim order. As soon as the application for an IVA has been lodged, application can be made ex parte for an order staying all actions against the debtor. Once this order has been made, any court in which proceedings are pending may stay those proceedings or allow them to continue on such terms as it thinks fit.

The application for an interim order must be accompanied by an affidavit setting out the reasons for making the application, details of all legal actions against the debtor and the fact that no previous application for an interim order has been made in the last 12 months. The court to which such an application has been made is the court that would have jurisdiction in bankruptcy. The application must be served on the nominee, any creditor who has presented a bankruptcy petition or, if the debtor is already bankrupt, his trustee.

If the court makes the order, it lasts for 14 days, but can be extended if the nominee asks for more time to file his report. On the making of an interim order, the court must fix a time and date for consideration of the nominees report. This date will also be the date when the interim report ceases to have effect. The nominees report must be filed two days before this hearing. Within seven days of delivering the proposal to his nominee, the debtor must also deliver a statement of his affairs. When the nominee lodges his report at court, he also delivers a copy of the debtors proposals and statements of affairs.

The nominees report and the debtors statement of affairs are heard in court, with the court either discharging the interim order or extending the period of the interim order if it feels that a meeting of creditors should be convened. If it goes this route, then the court will draw up the order and serve it on all parties with a meeting of the creditors being ordered which must be held between 14 and 28 days after the hearing.

At least 14 days notice must be given to all creditors The nominee will chair the subsequent meeting. After the creditors meeting, which is carried out by the usual rules governing such a meeting, contained within the Insolvency Act and outlined earlier in the book, there is a third hearing in court, at which the creditors report to the creditors meeting is considered. If the debtors proposal has been declined, the court will discharge the interim order and leave the debtor to the mercy of the creditors. If the meeting has approved the debtors proposal no further order will be made by the court but the IVA will now be in place.

If the debtor was an undischarged bankrupt, the effect of approval to an IVA is that the bankruptcy order against him can be annulled but only once the period during which an application to challenge the creditors decision could be made (28 days) has expired or after any application has been dealt with by the court and subject to any order of the court as to the termination of the administration of the bankruptcy.

The approved arrangement binds every person who has been given notice of the meeting of creditors and was entitled to vote at it. If a creditor has not been given notice of the meeting he can pursue his actions against the debtor including bankruptcy proceedings, though if the creditor could not, by virtue of the size of his debt, have materially affected the outcome of the meeting, the court may prefer to order that a fresh meeting be convened.

Now read the key points from Chapter Seven

## KEY POINTS FROM CHAPTER SEVEN

- An individual voluntary arrangement is an arrangement between an individual debtor and his creditors whereby the creditors agree either to accept something less than 100 pence in the pound or agree deferment of the time for payment of their debts.

- Only individual debtors can make proposals for an IVA. The Insolvency Act 1986 sets out the details that must be contained in the proposal.

- The debtor must apply to court for an interim order giving protection from his creditors. The order, if made, lasts for 14 days, but can be extended.

# 8
# INSOLVENT PARTNERSHIPS

The rules relating to insolvent partnerships are set out in the Insolvency Partnerships Order 1986 (CREDITORS). Schedules 1 and 2 to the CREDITORS deal with modifications of the Insolvency Act 1986 in their applications to insolvent partnerships. Schedule 3 sets out the prescribed forms. Insolvent partnerships are now treated as unregistered companies for the purpose of insolvency and are wound up accordingly. Individual partners can also be made the subject of individual bankruptcy orders or, if they are corporate members of a partnership, winding up orders. When a partnership is wound up, its assets are first used to meet partnership liabilities and then any surplus goes to meet any shortfall in the personal liabilities of the partners.

Similarly, the assets of partners are first used to meet their personal debts and then any surplus is used to meet the shortfall in the partnership liabilities. Priority of debts is dealt with in part 10 of the CREDITORS. Former partners in an insolvent partnership are liable to be disqualified from acting as directors of a company under the Company Directors Disqualification Act 1986 in the same way as directors of insolvent companies.

There are four alternative ways of dealing with insolvent companies:

* wind up the partnership;

* wind up the partnership and make the individual partners bankrupt (or in the case of a corporate partner, put into liquidation);

* wind up the partnership and make the individual partners bankrupt (or in the case of a corporate partner, put into liquidation);
* make the individual partners bankrupt without making any insolvency order against the partnership as such

* make one or more of the individual partners bankrupt without making all of them bankrupt and without making any insolvency order against the partnership.

**Winding up a partnership**

To wind up an insolvent partnership, a winding up petition should be presented. If the petition is based upon a statutory demand, that demand must be in form 4.1 in schedule 4 to the insolvency rules. There is no right to apply to have the demand set aside. The petition to wind up the insolvent partnership is the same as any petition to wind up an unregistered company, namely, form 4.2 with such modifications as required. The partners themselves can petition to wind up the partnership.

An individual partner can petition for the partnership to be wound up providing he obtains the leave of the court. Leave will be granted if he proves that either he has obtained judgement against the partnership for a debt of not less than £750, that he has taken all reasonable steps to enforce the judgement and has served the statutory demand in form 2 in Schedule 3 to the CREDITORS.

To wind up the partnership and make the individual partners bankrupt, at least three petitions will be issued. One petition will be to wind up the partnership and the other petitions will be against the two or more individual partners. The only ground for a petition against a partnership is that it is unable to pay debts as evidenced by a failure to pay a debt exceeding £750 and to comply with the statutory demand served on the partnership and the individual partners. The petition against the individual partners can be heard only after the hearing of the petition against the partnership.

## Partners own petition for a bankruptcy order

This is the equivalent of the debtors petition in the case of a partnership. It is used where it is not desired to make a winding up order against the partnership even though the partnership is insolvent, and will more often be used in the case of small partnerships. The petition is form 8 in Schedule 3 and must be signed by all the partners or, if signed by only some of them, an affidavit must be sworn showing that the consent of all partners is given.

The petition must be presented to the court that would have jurisdiction to wind up the partnership. A statement of affairs is lodged at a later date. Unlike in individual bankruptcy petitions, there is no provision for the appointment of an insolvency practitioner to consider the possibility of a voluntary arrangement and no certificate of summary administration can be issued even if it is only a small case. After a bankruptcy order has been made against the partners, they can propose a voluntary arrangement to their creditors.

A creditor owed money by a partnership can petition for a winding up of the partnership or petition for the bankruptcy of individual partners without joining the other partners.

Now read the key points from Chapter Eight.

## KEY POINTS FROM CHAPTER EIGHT

- The rules relating to insolvent partnerships are set out in the Insolvency Partnerships Order 1986 (Creditors).

- When a partnership is wound up, its assets are first used to meet partnership liabilities and then any surplus goes to meet any shortfall in the personal liabilities of partners.

- To wind up an insolvent partnership, a winding up petition should be presented.

- A partner can issue his own petition for a bankruptcy order.

# 9
# INSOLVENT ESTATES

The Administration of Insolvent Estates of Deceased Persons Order 1986 (S1 no 1999) governs the administration of the affairs of deceased debtors. There are three situations where insolvency of an estate occurs:

* where administration has begun and it is discovered that the estate is insolvent, insolvent being the state of not being able to meet debts when the due or having a surplus of debts over liabilities

* where a bankruptcy petition is pending against the deceased at the time of his death

* where no administration has been applied for when a creditor begins to press.

where an estate is being administered and it is discovered that the estate is insolvent, the administration continues as before but the same provisions as are in force under the law of bankruptcy must be applied to the administration of the estate as regards the rights of creditors, provable debts and the priority of debts. There are two exceptions to this general rule. First, reasonable funeral, testamentary and administration expenses have priority over all other debts. Secondly, it is not necessary for the executors to be licensed insolvency practitioners. Even where no grant of probate has been obtained but where an application for such a grant is pending, the above rules apply but the court dealing with the application can transfer the proceedings to the appropriate bankruptcy court which can make an insolvency administration order.

If there is a bankruptcy petition pending against a debtor at the time of his death, the bankruptcy proceedings can continue as if he were still alive subject to certain modifications. One modification is that reasonable funeral and testamentary expenses have priority over the preferential debts. If the bankruptcy petition has not been served at the date of death, it can be served on the debtors personal representatives. The personal representatives can be required to do those things which the debtor himself is require to do under the bankruptcy rules.

Where there is no application for a grant of probate pending, a creditor can issue a petition for an insolvency administration order. The form of petition is form 1 in schedule 3 to the Order. The petition must be served on the personal representatives of the deceased unless the court orders otherwise.

A creditors petition for an insolvency administration order is form 1 schedule 3, unless the petition is presented following an individual voluntary arrangement in which case it is in form 2 to schedule 3 or as a result of criminal bankruptcy where it is in form 3 in schedule 3. If the personal representatives of the deceased wish to petition, they must use form 6 and they are required to lodge a statement of affairs at that time.

Now read the key points from Chapter Nine.

KEY POINTS FROM CHAPTER NINE

- The Administration of Insolvent Estates of Deceased Persons Order 1986 governs the administration of the affairs of deceased debtors.

- Reasonable funeral, testementary and administrative expenses have priority over all other debts.

- If there is a bankruptcy petition pending against a debtor at the time of his death, the bankruptcy proceedings can continue as if he were still alive subject to certain criteria.

# 10
# COMPULSORY LIQUIDATION

## Compulsory liquidation

The High Court alone has jurisdiction in winding up proceedings if the issued share capital of a company is in excess of £120,000. Proceedings can either be commenced in the Companies Court in London or at one of the eight provincial district registries with chancery jurisdiction. Enquiries can be made of a central register to see whether a winding up petition is pending.

The county court in the district in which the company is operating also has jurisdiction in winding up proceedings if the share capital does not exceed £120,000. In London, no county courts have bankruptcy jurisdiction.

If the petition is presented in the wrong court, the court can transfer the proceedings or allow the proceedings to continue where they are, providing the court has winding up jurisdiction. The court can also strike out proceedings.

## Preparing and serving the statutory demand

Like the demand served on an individual, a statutory demand served on a company is in prescribed form requiring the debtor to pay the debt contained within the demand or secure or compound the debt to the creditors satisfaction within the period of three weeks after the demand has been served.

The demand must exceed £750, its purpose to show that the company cannot meet its liabilities. The demand can be from one or more persons. The form of statutory demand is prescribed by schedule 4 to the rules, form 4.1. A petition can also be based on an unsatisfied execution or on the inability of the company to pay debts-in which there is no minimum debt requirement. The demand must be left at the registered office of the company. Service by post is not available unless the debtor-company acknowledges that the demand was received.

**Creditors petitions**

The petition must be presented to either the High court or to the appropriate county court. A petition to wind up a company may be presented to a court if the company has, by resolution resolved that the company be wound up by a court or the company is unable to meet its debts or it is "just and equitable" that the company be wound up.

A company is deemed unable to pay its debts if a creditor has served a statutory demand for the minimum amount and the company has neglected to pay the sum or to secure or compound it within three weeks after service of the demand. If the execution or other process against the company is returned unsatisfied in whole or in part (no minimum debt requirement), then a company is also deemed to be unable to pay its debts.

A company is also deemed unable to pay its debts if its liabilities exceed its assets. A statutory demand does not have to have been served on a company for a petition to be presented for its winding up. If the debt is due and unpaid, and cannot be disputed on a substantial ground, then this is evidence that there is an inability to pay.

There is a prescribed form of petition (form 4.2) set out in schedule 4 to the rules.

If two or more creditors are jointly petitioning, all their details must be given. Secured creditors must value their security and can only petition for the unsecured part of their debt. The petition must state the amount of the debt and the consideration for it.

Every petition must be verified by an affidavit. The affidavit must exhibit a copy of the petition.

On the issue of a petition, the following are required:

* petition together with copies for service on the company and any other party, such as administrator, administrative receiver, supervisor or voluntary liquidator

* affidavit verifying the petition

* receipt for the deposit payable to the official   receiver

* The fee-see current county and high court fees.

All copies of the petition are sealed by the court except for one, and handed back to the petitioner. The petition is endorsed with time date and place of the court hearing. At least one director of the company must receive a sealed copy or a person authorised to receive it. It can be left at the registered office. If none of these methods of service are utilised, or can be utilised, then the court may allow substituted service on an ex parte application. If a voluntary arrangement is in force, the supervisor must be served as well as the company unless it is the supervisor who is petitioning. If an administrative receiver has been appointed, that person must also be served If the company is already in voluntary liquidation, the voluntary liquidator must be served.

The petition must be advertised in the London Gazette not less than seven business days before the hearing and not less than seven business days after service. The form of advertisement is prescribed (form 4.6)

All creditors, directors and shareholders of the company are entitled to be furnished with a copy of the petition within two days of requesting the same on payment of a fee.

The petitioner or his solicitor must lodge a certificate showing compliance with the rules, together with the gazette advertisement, at least five business days before the hearing. Petitions are initially set down for hearing before a registrar of the company's court in London or a district judge (of the High Court or county court) elsewhere. If the petition is opposed, it must be adjourned to a High court or circuit judge. Any creditor who intends to appear on the hearing of the petition must give notice to the petitioning creditor. The notice must state the amount of debt and whether he intends to support or oppose the petition. The petitioning creditor must prepare a list of the creditors who have given notice to appear. The courts will generally look at the list of those who oppose and support the petition and the quality of the list before making a decision. It does not automatically follow that it will be dismissed if there are opponents.

If the petitioning creditor has received his monies, another creditor may be substituted for him. A petition cannot be withdrawn except for leave of the court. If a petition has been served but not advertised and the company consents, leave to withdraw will be given on an ex parte application providing that this is applied for at least five days before the hearing.

**The hearing of the petition**

On the hearing of the petition the court may make a winding up order, adjourn the hearing conditionally or unconditionally or dismiss the petition. The general rule is that if there are a majority of creditors in value supporting a petition, then a winding up order will be made. An order that the costs of the petitioning creditor be paid out of the assets of the company will usually be made by the court. These costs are a first charge on the companies assets and rank ahead of all other claims of secured creditors (including a fixed charge).

The winding up order (form 4.11 in schedule 4) is then drafted by the court and a draft is sent to the petitioning creditor or his solicitors who will engross the draft and then return it to the court for sealing (together with sufficient copies). The court sends three sealed copies to the Official Receiver who in turn will serve a copy on the company and the Registrar of Companies and arranges for the order to be advertised. The court will also inform the Official Receiver of the making of the order immediately after it has been made. If the petition is dismissed, the court will draft the order and submit it to the petitioning creditor or his solicitor for engrossment.

**Before and after a company winding up**

If a company goes into liquidation, any disposition of its property (including payments made by it) after the date of the presentation of the petition is void (unless made with the consent of, or subsequently ratified by, the court). Once a winding up petition has been presented, the court may stay any action or other legal process against the debtor or his property. The granting of a stay is discretionary. If the proceedings are pending in the High court, that court may stay the proceedings. Otherwise application must be made to the court dealing with the winding up petition. Any attachment, distress or execution issued against the company is also void and a creditor who, prior to the date of presentation of the petition, issued an attachment or execution which remained incomplete at that date cannot retain the benefit of his action. A distraining creditor can retain the benefit of his distraint.

Once a winding up order has been made or a provisional liquidator has been appointed, no creditor of the company may commence any action against the company without leave of the court. This rule does not affect the right of a creditor to the benefit of executions completed before the presentation of the winding up petition.

Executions are complete when goods have been sold and proceeds held by the sheriff or bailiff for at least 14 days, when a charging order absolute has been obtained or when a debt garnished has been paid. A secured creditor is not affected by these provisions and can enforce his security though he cannot take any action in connection with any unsecured shortfall.

**Appointment of a provisional liquidator**

If it is necessary to protect the company's property prior to the hearing of the winding up petition, the court can, on the application of the company, the petitioner or creditor, appoint the official receiver or some other fit person. The court will specify the powers that the provisional liquidator will have.

Every court having jurisdiction in winding up proceedings may review, rescind or vary any order made by it. An application to rescind must normally be made within seven days, though the court will normally extend the time for applying in appropriate cases. If the proceedings have been transferred from one court to another after the making of the winding up order, the transferee court can also exercise this power.

In all cases where a winding up order is made and later the appointment of a provisional liquidator, the directors or other officers of the company are obliged to submit a statement of affairs. The statement must be submitted to the official receiver within 21 days of the making of the winding up order or the appointment of a provisional liquidator or such longer time as the court or the Official Receiver may allow.

The statement must contain full particulars of the company's creditors, debts and other liabilities and of its assets together with such information as may be prescribed. Form 4.17 (in Schedule 4 to the rules) is the prescribed form for the statement of affairs. The official receiver is obliged to give to the persons making the statement of affairs a copy of the form. The official receiver may himself employ someone to assist the deponents with the statement of affairs, paid for out of the assets of the company.

**Public examination**

The Official Receiver may make an application to the court for the public examination of the former officers to be held. The Official receiver must make an application for a public examination if requested to do so by half in value of the creditors or 75% of the contributors. If the examinee fails to attend the public examination without reasonable excuse, he is guilty of contempt of court.

At the public examination, the official receiver, the liquidator, any creditor who has tendered a proof of debt or any contributory can ask questions and can with the approval of the court, appear by solicitor or counsel or authorise in writing another person to question the bankrupt on his behalf. The person being examined is entitled to legal representation. If criminal proceedings have commenced against a director and the court is of the opinion that the continuation of the examination would be likely to prejudice a fair trial of those proceedings, the examination may be adjourned.

The court may order any former officer of the company or any person thought to have information relating to the property of the company to attend court and to answer questions. If the person does not attend he can be arrested and brought before the court.

**Appointing a liquidator**

The Official Receiver is liquidator until someone else is appointed. A liquidator can be appointed by a general meeting of the creditors, the court or by the Secretary of State. Only an authorised insolvency practitioner can act as liquidator. The Official Receiver must decide within 12 weeks of the making of the winding up order whether or not to summon a meeting of the creditors and appoint a liquidator. 21 days notice should be given to creditors of such a meeting. Notice must also be given in local newspapers and the London Gazette. The Official Receiver will act as chair of the first meeting and the liquidator at all other meetings. Resolutions are deemed to be passed on a majority in value of creditors and contributors present personally or by proxy. There has to be a quorum present that consists of at least one creditor.

The primary purpose at the first meeting is to appoint a liquidator. No resolution can be proposed which suggests the Official Receiver as the liquidator. The Official Receiver will remain the liquidator only if another is not proposed and the Official Receiver does not ask the Secretary of State to be liquidator. No person can be appointed as liquidator unless he is a qualified insolvency practitioner.

Creditors can resolve to establish a liquidation committee but a committee cannot be established at any time when the Official Receiver is liquidator. Any creditor other than a secured creditor is eligible to be a member of the committee. A body corporate can be a member of the committee but can only act through a representative. A creditors committee must consist of at least three and not more than five members.

The role of the committee is primarily supervisory. It determines the liquidators remuneration. The liquidator is under a duty to report to the committee all matters of concern to it in relation to the administration of the estate. The first meeting of the committee must take place within three months of its establishment and thereafter within 21 days of a request for a meeting by a committee member. The quorum for the meeting is two. The liquidator can seek to obtain the agreement of the committee to a resolution by sending to every member a copy of the proposed resolution.

Now read the key points from Chapter Ten

## KEY POINTS FROM CHAPTER TEN

- The High Court alone has jurisdiction in winding up proceedings if the issued share capital of a company is in excess of £20,000.

- A Statutory demand must be served on the company giving three weeks to comply. The demand must exceed £750. The following petition must be presented to the appropriate court.

- At least one director of the company must receive a sealed copy of the petition or a person authorised to receive it. Petitions are initially set down for a hearing before a registrar of the Companies Court in London or a District Judge. On the hearing, the court may make a winding up order, adjourn the hearing or dismiss the petition.

- If it is necessary to protect the company's property, prior to the hearing, a court can appoint the Official Receiver to do so.

# 11
# CREDITORS VOLUNTARY LIQUIDATION

## Members voluntary liquidation

This chapter deals with creditors voluntary liquidations and not members voluntary liquidations that come about when the shareholders of the company wish the company to be liquidated in circumstances other than its insolvency. Even though a company which is placed into member's voluntary liquidation is not insolvent, only a licensed insolvency practitioner can be the liquidator.

If a company goes into members voluntary liquidation and it subsequently transpires that the company is insolvent, then a meeting of creditors must be convened similar to a meeting under s98 (see below) and to receive a statement of affairs and to consider whether or not the liquidators should continue in office.

## Creditors voluntary liquidation

When it appears to the directors that a company cannot continue to trade by reason of its insolvency, the directors can resolve to convene meetings of its shareholders and creditors to consider and, if thought fit, to pass a resolution that the company be wound up. The shareholders meeting must be convened in accordance with the memorandum and articles of association of the company and the Companies Act 1985. The creditors meeting is governed by the Insolvency Act 1986 s98. At least seven days notice of the meeting must be given to creditors.

The meeting must be advertised in the London Gazette and local newspapers. The creditors meeting must be held not more than 14 days after the shareholders meeting, though both meetings are usually held on the same day. A list of creditors must be available for inspection in the locality where the company traded or an insolvency practitioner must be named who can provide a list of names on request.

The purpose of the meeting is to resolve to put the company into liquidation and to appoint a liquidator and a liquidation committee. If a company has already been placed in members voluntary liquidation and it appears to the liquidator that all the creditors debts will not be paid, in full or part, or within 12 months of the liquidation commencing, he must call meetings of creditors in much the same way as meetings under s 98.

It is the duty of directors to nominate one of their number to chair meetings and to lay before the meeting a statement of affairs. The shareholders at the meeting not only resolve that the company proceed to voluntary liquidation but also nominate someone to act as liquidator. If the creditors at their meeting make no fresh nominations, the shareholders nominee as liquidator will be confirmed in office.

The liquidator must advertise his appointment in a local newspaper and also lodge a notice of his appointment with the registrar of local companies. The liquidator can ask directors to produce accounts and can provide for the cost of the preparation out of the company's assets. The liquidator is obliged to give all creditors within 28 days of the meeting a copy of the statement of affairs and a report of what took place at the meeting.

# 12
# ALL LIQUIDATIONS

## The powers of the liquidator

The liquidator may disclaim any property of the company that is onerous. This is property that is unsaleable or may give rise to a liability to pay money or perform any other onerous task on behalf of the company. In order to disclaim the liquidator must give a notice in the prescribed form (form 4.53 in schedule 4 to the rules), file at court the notice and serve the same on the party affected. If the liquidator disclaims a lease, the court can vest the property in any person claiming an interest in that property, the guarantor of any liability in respect of the property or, in the case of a dwelling house, the occupant.

Disclaimer operates so as to determine the rights, interests and liabilities of the company in respect of a disclaimed property. Disclaimer does not affect the rights and liabilities of third parties except in so far as necessary in releasing the company from any liability. Accordingly, a guarantor of a lease disclaimed by the liquidator is released from any further liability as from the date of the disclaimer unless the company was only an assignee of the lease.

## Mutual credit and sell off

An account must be taken of what sum is due from the company to a person with whom there have been mutual credits, mutual debts or other dealings. The sum due from one party must be set off against the sum due from the other and only the balance of the account is provable in the liquidation or is to be paid to the liquidator for the benefit of all creditors. For set off to be allowed, there must be obligations on both side giving rise to pecuniary liabilities so that an account can be taken and a balance struck. If the obligation on the one side is to deliver goods and on the other is to pay a sum of money, there can be no set off.

For set off to be successful, both liabilities must have arisen prior to the commencement of the liquidation even though one of the debts may not be immediately due and not enforceable until a time after the liquidation began. There can be no set off between separate debts and joint debts. Debts must be due in the same right. Set off will not be allowed where credit was given to the same company by a creditor who had knowledge of the calling of a creditors meeting under s98 or of the presentation of a winding up petition.

If a creditor has to pay money to a liquidator he cannot set off against the sum he is required to pay any sum due to him from the company. Right to set off may exist even though one of the debts may be secured.

**General control of the liquidator**

There are many powers which the liquidator can exercise only with permission of a liquidation committee or, if there is no committee, with permission of the Secretary of State. Some powers can be exercised without sanction in a voluntary liquidation but only with sanction in a winding up by the court. These powers are set out in ss 165 and 166 (voluntary liquidation) and s167 (winding up by the court) and schedule 4:

* carrying on the business of the company

* instituting or defending any legal actions (in a winding up by the court)

* compromising any claim by the company against a third party: and

* compromising any dispute with the company's creditors.

The liquidator may, without the permission of the liquidation committee, sell the company's property and borrow money on the security of the company's assets. If the liquidator does anything which requires permission but without obtaining that permission, his actions can be ratified if the committee is satisfied that he acted in a case of urgency and applied to the committee without undue delay.

The liquidator does not require the committee's sanction to employ a solicitor. He should, however, give notice of his actions to the liquidation committee. The liquidator has power to summon meetings of creditors so as to ascertain creditor's wishes. Creditors have the right to apply to court for any decision of the liquidator to be reversed or modified if they are dissatisfied. The liquidators remuneration is determined by the liquidation committee but if the liquidator is not satisfied with the decision of the committee, he can call a meeting of the creditors to resolve otherwise. If still not satisfied he can apply to the court.

Similarly, creditors can apply to the court to reduce liquidators charges. The liquidation committee can require the liquidator to insist that his solicitors fees be taxed notwithstanding that he is of the opinion that they are reasonable.

The liquidator is subject to control by the court on the application of any creditor or contributory. The liquidator is subject to control by the Department of Trade on the monetary aspects of his administration.

The liquidator in a winding up by the court is required to pay all the monies into the insolvency services account at the Bank of England within 14 days of receipt of funds. In a voluntary liquidation he must pay any monies received by him and undistributed after six months into the insolvency services account at the Bank of England.

He is also obliged to send to the Secretary of State an account of all his receipts and payments every year. The court will not allow the liquidator in a winding up by the court to retain or claim monies for distribution among the creditors when it would be inconsistent with natural justice to do so and something which an honest man would not do.

## Adjustment of prior transactions

The kind of matters liable to be set aside are transactions at an under-value or preferences. The liquidator has the power to apply to the court for the reversal of certain transactions if they were to the disadvantage of the company and were carried out at a "relevant time". The relevant time is defined in s240 in relation to transactions at an undervalue or a preference as being any time in the two years preceding the onset of insolvency but, in the case of preferences not benefiting a connected person, at any time in the period of six months prior to the onset of insolvency.

Transactions cannot be set aside if the company was able to pay its debts at the time of the events or became unable to do so as a result. A company is deemed to be unable to pay its debts if it has failed to comply with a statutory demand served on it, or has allowed execution to go unsatisfied or if its liabilities exceed its assets at any one time.

Where a company entered into a transaction at an under value at a relevant time, the court can order the return of the benefit. For an order to be made, the court must be satisfied that the company had entered into a transaction.

Where a creditor has, before the commencement of the winding up, issued execution against the goods or land of the company or attached any debt due to it, he cannot retain the benefit of his actions as against the liquidator unless execution or attachment was completed prior to the commencement of the winding up. All forms for distraint are subject to the rule that if they have taken place in the three months prior to the making of the winding up order, the proceeds of the distraint are 'charged' with the preferential debt.

No lien or other right to possession of any books, papers or other records of the company is enforceable against the liquidator.

## Debts and dividends

There are four classes of creditor-secured, preferential, unsecured or deferred. A secured creditor is not given any special priority by the Act or the Rules but can rely on his security. He may, with the agreement of the liquidator and leave of the court, at any time alter the value which he has, in the proof of his debt, placed on his security, though if he petitioned for the winding up of his company or has voted in respect of his unsecured balance he may only re-value his security with leave of the court.

If a secured creditor omits to disclose his security in his proof of debt, he must surrender it for the general benefit of creditors unless the court relieves him on the ground that omission was a mistake. A liquidator may redeem the security of the value placed on it by the creditor if he so wishes and a secured creditor has the right to call on the liquidator to elect whether or not to exercise this power.

Preferential debts are defined in s386 and schedule 6 to the Act. They consist primarily of taxes such as PAYE, VAT and social security contributions. Amounts due to employees for wages for the four months prior to the making of the winding up order or resolution to wind up but not exceeding £800 for each employee are preferential, together with all arrears of holiday pay. If monies have been advanced by a third party to pay wages and holiday pay which otherwise would have been preferential debts, then the person who advanced the money becomes a preferential creditor for the amount advanced.

Unsecured creditors are the ordinary debts of the company which are neither secured nor preferential.

## Provable debts

All claims by creditors against the company are provable in the liquidation whether they are present or future, certain or contingent, ascertained or sounding in damages. Even unliquidated damages of tort are provable debts.

## Proofs of debt

Every person claiming to be a creditor in a winding up by the court must submit his claim in writing to the Official Receiver or the liquidator-this is called proving his debt. In voluntary liquidation, formal proofs of debts are not usually required-a claim in any form is sufficient but the liquidator can call for a formal proof of debt to be submitted. A proof of debt must be in the prescribed form (form 4.25 in schedule 4 to the rules) or a substantially similar form.

Proof of debts forms must be sent out by the Official Receiver or liquidator to every creditor who is known to him or identified in the statement of affairs. The liquidator may require a proof of debt to be verified by affidavit in form 4.26. A proof of debt must contain details of the creditors name and address, the amount owing, the date of the liquidation, the date of the liquidation, whether interest and VAT is included, whether any part of the debt is preferential, how the debt was incurred and particulars of any security held and its value.

There is no time limit for the submission of proofs of debt but a creditor who has not proved his debt cannot benefit from any distribution prior to proof. Before declaring a dividend, the liquidator must give notice of his intention to do so to all creditors of whom he is aware and who have not proved their debts. The notice must specify the last date for proving which must not be less than 21 days after the date of the notice and must state the liquidators intention to declare a dividend.

The liquidator cannot declare a dividend until he has examined every proof of debt. If a creditor is dissatisfied at the decision of the liquidator, the court may reverse that decision.

**Interest**

When a debt proved in a liquidation bears interest the proof of debt can include interest up to the date of the liquidation. If the debt does not include the right to interest, interest can none the less be claimed up to the date of liquidation.

**VAT**

A creditor whose claim includes an element of VAT can either prove for the whole amount of the claim (and pay to Customs and Excise the VAT element irrespective of whether or not he receives any dividend) or prove for the amount of his claim net of VAT and reclaim the VAT. No formalities are required to reclaim the VAT element of the debt owed by the bankrupt-the creditor is automatically entitled to VAT bad debt relief once he has written off the debt in his books and the debt is no more than six months old.

**Dividends**

The liquidator must give notice of a dividend to all creditors who have proved their debts. the notice must include details of the amounts realised from the sale of the assets, payments made by the liquidator in his administration, the total amount distributed, the rate of dividend and whether any further dividends are to be expected. The liquidator must not, except with the leave of the court, proceed to declare a dividend where there is a pending application to vary a decision of his on a proof of debt.

If the liquidator is unable to declare any or any further dividend, he must give notice to this effect to creditors. A creditor who has failed to lodge his proof of debt before an interim dividend was declared is not entitled to disturb that interim distribution but is entitled to receive a payment in priority to other creditors from further funds available.

The liquidator cannot be sued for a dividend but if he refuses to pay a dividend the court may order him to pay it together with, out of his own funds, interest at judgement rate and costs. When the liquidator is ready to close his administration, he must give notice to the creditors of his intention to declare a final dividend or that no further dividend will be declared. The notice must require any remaining claims to be established by a certain date: if they are not, they can be ignored by the liquidator.

Now read the key points from Chapter Twelve.

KEY POINTS FROM CHAPTER TWELVE

- The liquidator may disclaim any property of the company that is onerous. Disclaimer does not affect the rights and liabilities of third parties.

- There are many powers that the liquidator can exercise with the permission of a liquidation committee or Secretary of State. The liquidator may sell the company's property and borrow money on the security of the company's assets without permission of the committee or Secretary of State.

- All claims by creditors are provable.

- The liquidator must give notice of a dividend to all creditors who have proved their debts.

# 13
# RECEIVERSHIPS

## Nature of receivership

There are three kinds of receivership-under the Law of Property Act in respect of a property, by the court and by a debenture holder under a floating charge debenture. Court appointed receivers are rare. If a receiver is appointed under a floating charge debenture, he is called an administrative receiver. This chapter relates to administrative receivers.

The appointment of a receiver is of no effect unless it is accepted by the receiver before the end of the next business day. Acceptance must be in writing or confirmed in writing before seven days. The receiver may apply to court for directions in relation to any matter arising in connection with the performance of his functions. The court can fix the receivers remuneration if asked to do so by the liquidator of the company. The receiver must make it clear, on each invoice and other paperwork, that a receiver has been appointed.

A receiver is personally liable on any contract entered into by him and even in relation to any contract of employment adopted by him, though he is entitled to indemnity out of the assets of the company.

## Priority of debts in receivership

If an asset is subject to a fixed charge, the receiver need have regard to no debts in priority to those owed to the fixed charge holder. If assets are subject only to a floating charge, then the receiver must ensure that the preferential creditors of the company are paid in full before the debenture holder receives any payment. Preferential creditors are defined in schedule 6 of the Act. If there is a surplus from the sale of a fixed charge asset after paying off the amount due to the chargee, the surplus must not be used for the payment of preferential creditors but handed on to any liquidator subsequently appointed.

## Powers of the receiver

The powers confirmed on a receiver are set out in schedule 1 to the Act and include the right to take or defend proceedings in the companies name, sell the companies assets, borrow money, appoint solicitors, use the company seal, carry on business and even petition for the winding up of the company. The receiver has power to apply to the court to allow the disposal of an asset subject to a fixed charge as if that asset were not subject to such security. This is in order to prevent a creditor owed more than the value of his security preventing beneficial realisation of the company's assets.

An English receiver's powers extend to assets in Scotland and vice versa.

## Duties of a receiver

The receiver is under an obligation to notify the company and advertise notice of his appointment and within 28 days to send a similar notice to all creditors of the company. Every receiver or manager of a company's property must deliver to the Registrar of Companies an account of his receipts and payments every twelve months. An administrative receiver must report to creditors within three months after his appointment and send to the Registrar of Companies and to all creditors a report of the events leading up to his appointment, details of what property is being disposed by him, the amount owed to the debenture holders and to preferential creditors and the amount, if any, likely to be available to ordinary creditors.

A copy of his report must also be given to a meeting of the company's ordinary creditors within the same time-scale.

The meeting of the creditors can decide to establish a committee "to assist the receiver". The committee can require the receiver to attend meetings and to provide it with information. The rules governing the above are to found in s46-49. The rules governing the conduct of the creditors meeting in a receivership are contained in rr 3.9-3.15. The functions of the creditors committee are to assist the receiver and to act as agreed with him.

## Statement of affairs

After an administrative receiver has been appointed, the directors of the company are under an obligation to submit a statement of affairs (s47). The statement should be in form 3.2 in schedule 4 to the rules and must be verified by affidavit. The court can order limited disclosure of the information contained in the statement of affairs or even release the directors from the obligation to submit such a statement.

## VAT

No formalities are required to reclaim the VAT element of the debt owed by the bankrupt-the creditor is automatically entitled to VAT bad debt relief once he has written off the debt in his books and the debt is more than six months old.

Now read the key points from Chapter Thirteen.

# KEY POINTS FROM CHAPTER THIRTEEN

- There are three kinds of receivership-under the Law of Property Act, in respect of a court order or by a debenture holder.

- Fixed charge assets are given priority by the receiver. All debts are prioritised.

- An English receivers powers extend to assets in Scotland and Vice versa.

- A receiver must report to all creditors within three months. After a receiver has been appointed, directors of a company are under an obligation to submit a statement of affairs.

# 14
# COMPANY VOLUNTARY ARRANGEMENTS

## Nature of a company voluntary arrangement (CVA)

A CVA is an agreement between a company and its shareholders and creditors. There is little court involvement. It is only necessary for copies of certain documents to be lodged at court so as to be available for public inspection. Only an authorised insolvency practitioner may be the nominee and supervisor in a CVA. A CVA can be proposed even after a company has gone into administration or liquidation. The object of a CVA can either be a moratorium (a delay of payment until a certain event happens or payment by instalment) or the payment of less than 100p in the pound in full settlement.

The directors of a company, the liquidator or administrator can make a proposal for a CVA. (s1). The proposal must contain an explanation why a CVA is desirable and why the company's creditors might be expected to agree with it. the proposal must set out details of the companies assets and liabilities, how it is proposed to deal with secured and preferential creditors and creditors who are connected to the company, whether there are any circumstances that might give rise to an adjustment of prior transactions, what costs were involved in the CVA, what duties the supervisor will undertake and so on.

If it is the directors who are putting forward the proposal, they must select an authorised insolvency practitioner to act as nominee. It is the nominees duty to report to the creditors (and to the court) on the directors proposals (r17). The proposers of the proposal must give to the nominee a statement of affairs relating to the company (r1.5) and all these documents must be lodged in court. If the nominee is of the opinion that there is some prospect of the CVA being approved, he will state that in his opinion a meeting of the shareholders and the creditors of the company should be convened to consider the proposal.

## Meetings of shareholders and creditors

For a CVA to be approved, shareholders and creditors must give their approval. The shareholders meeting must be held on the same day but after the creditors meeting. The rules as to the conduct of the meeting are contained in rr 1.14-1.16. For a CVA to be approved, there has to be a 75% majority in favour of it. The majority is calculated by reference to the value of the creditor's claims of those creditors present in person or by proxy and voting at the meeting. Shareholders approval is given by simple majority.

If any shareholder or creditor feels that the meetings have not been conducted in accordance with the rules or that the interests of a shareholder or member have been unfairly prejudiced by the CVA, he may apply to the court for revocation or suspension of the CVA (s6). The court can order further meetings to be held.

An approved CVA binds everyone who was given notice of, and was entitled to vote at, the meeting to consider the proposal whether or not he was actually present at that meeting. If the company is in administration or liquidation, the court may stay the proceedings and give directions with regard to the proceedings as are appropriate for facilitating the implementation of the CVA (s5 (3)). The winding up of the company is, however, not rescinded or reversed but simply stayed. The person whose function it is to carry out the CVA is the supervisor. He may apply to the court for directions in relation to any matters arising in the CVA and also to wind up the company if necessary.

Once a CVA is approved, the directors must do everything that is required for putting the supervisor into possession of the assets included in the arrangement. The supervisor has an obligation to keep accounts and records of his dealings and to prepare an account of all his receipts and payments not less than once every twelve months and send it to the courts, the registrar of companies, shareholders and creditors. The supervisor must also produce to the Secretary of State his records and accounts if so requested. Not more than 28 days after the final completion of the CVA the supervisor must send to all shareholders and creditors a notice that the CVA has been fully implemented, and lodge a copy with the court.

Now read the key points from Chapter 14.

## KEY POINTS FROM CHAPTER FOURTEEN

- A compulsory voluntary arrangement is between a company and its shareholders and creditors. There is little court involvement. Only an authorised insolvency practitioner may be the nominee and supervisor.

- The directors of a company, the liquidator or the administrator can make a proposal for a CVA.

- For a CVA to be approved, shareholders and creditors must give their approval.

- An approved CVA binds everyone who was given notice of, and was entitled to vote at, the meeting to consider the proposal whether or not they were present at the meeting.

# 15
# ADMINISTRATION

## Nature of administration

Administrations were introduced into insolvency legislation to enable those appointed as administrator to run the business as a going concern, and promote the rehabilitation of that business. The purposes for which an administration order can be made are (s8(3)):

* the survival of the company in whole or in part as a going concern

* the approval of a voluntary arrangement

* the sanctioning of a scheme under the Companies Act s 425 or

* a more advantageous realisation of the companies assets than would be the case in a winding up.

The court can make an administration order only if it is satisfied that the company is insolvent and that one of the purposes set out above would likely to be achieved (s8).

## Application for an administration order (s9)

An application for an administration order is made by petition either by the company, all the company's directors, creditors or the supervisor. The petition should be in form 2.1 in schedule 4 to the rules and must be supported by an affidavit together with the proposed administrator's report where available.

The petition is presented to the court having jurisdiction to wind up the company, that is, the county court for the area where the registered office is situated if the share capital is less than £120,000, or the High Court (be it in London or one of the eight provincial district registries). The petition must be served on the company, anyone entitled to appoint an administrative receiver, the administrative receiver if one has been appointed and the proposed administrator.

The effect of an application for an administration order is that no steps can be taken in legal actions or executions against the company or its property except with leave of the court and no steps can be taken to enforce any security over the company's property while the application is pending, again except with leave of the court. Also, the company may not resolve to wind up while the application is pending. The court has power to make an interim order once an application has been lodged. The court must not make an administration order if an administrative receiver has been appointed unless the appointer consents.

On the hearing of the application, anyone entitled to appoint an administrative receiver may appear together with the petitioner of the company itself. In addition, with the leave of the court, anyone else who appears to have an interest may appear. It is the court that appoints the administrator though the administrator is nominated by the applicant for the order. The administration order must specify the one or more purposes set out in s 8(3) which the administration order is intended to achieve. The form of order is form 2.4 in schedule four to the rules.

Once an administration order is made, any petition for the winding up of the company is dismissed automatically and any administrative receiver must vacate office. Also, no resolution for the voluntary winding up of the company can be passed, no administrative receiver may be appointed and no steps may be taken in any legal proceedings against the company or for enforcement of any security over the company's assets except with leave of the court.

## Powers of the administrator

The powers of the administrator are set out in schedule 1 to the Act. These powers are the same as for an administrative receiver and include the powers to sell the company's property, to bring or defend proceedings in the company's name etc.

However, no sale of the company's property can be effected by an administrator until he has put proposals to the creditors and a creditors meeting has been held, unless the matter is one of urgency.

## Power to deal with charged property

An administrator may dispose of any charged property as if the property were not subject to any security, if the court is satisfied that the disposal of that property would be likely to promote one ore more of the purposes specified in the administration order (s15(1) and (2). Where property is disposed of under s 15(1) the holder of this security has the same priority in respect of the proceeds of sale as he had over the property disposed of.

It is a condition of the court granting an order under s 15(1) that the net proceeds of sale and, where the proceeds of sale are less than the amount which would have been realised on a sale in the open market, the sums which are required to make good a deficiency be paid towards discharging the sums due to the secured creditor.

Section 15 applies equally to goods the subject of hire purchase agreements and goods the subject of retention of title claims. Rule 2.51 sets out the procedure for making the application.

## Summoning creditors meetings

The administrator must convene a meeting of creditors if requested to do so by 10% in value of the creditors or if directed to do so by the courts. An administrator must also convene a meeting of creditors to consider his proposals under s23 (below).

## Discharge or variation of the administration order

The administrator may at any time apply to the court for the administration order to be discharged or varied (s18 (1). He must make an application for the order to be discharged or varied if it appears to him that the purposes(s) of the order have been achieved or incapable of achievement.

If an administration order is discharged, the administrator will be released from all liability in respect of his conduct only if the court orders. Where a winding up order is made immediately on the discharge of an administration order, the court may appoint as liquidator the person who had been the administrator, but only after that person has informed the creditors of his intention to ask the court to appoint him as liquidator.

## Investigation by the administrator

The directors are under a duty (s22) to submit to the administrator a statement of affairs relating to the company, verified by affidavit. Limited disclosure or even release from the obligation to submit a statement of affairs may be ordered by the court or allowed by the administrator. The administrator is under a duty to report to the DTI any conduct of the officers of the company that might merit their disqualification from acting as directors.

The administrator is under a duty to lay before a meeting of creditors, within three months of his appointment, his proposals. He must serve copies on all shareholders and advertise. Within the proposal must be a statement setting out details of his appointment or the purpose for which it was made, a copy of the statement of affairs and such other information as would be necessary to enable creditors to decide whether or not to vote for the adoption of the proposal. At the meeting, creditors will decide whether or not to approve the administrator proposals.

The administrator must report the outcome of the meeting to the court and if the report states that the meeting has declined to approve the administrator's proposals, the court may discharge the administration order. The rules as to the conduct of the meeting are set out in r 2.1 (8) - 2.25 (5) and are the usual rules that apply to all meetings of creditors under the insolvency legislation.

Where the administrators proposals have been approved and the administrator proposes to make revisions to these proposals, he must inform all creditors of his proposed revisions and convene a further meeting of creditors on not less than 14 days notice (s25).

Where a meeting of creditors has been convened under s 23 and has approved the administrators proposals, the meeting may, if it thinks fit, establish a creditors committee (s26 (1) ). The functions of the committee are to assist the administrator and to act in relation to him in such a manner as may be agreed from time to time.

At any time when an administration order is in force, a creditor or shareholder may apply to the court for an order on the grounds that his interests have been unfairly prejudiced or that any act or omission of the administrator would be prejudicial to his interests. On such an application the court can make an order regulating the future management by the administrator, requiring the summoning of a meeting of creditors or even discharging the administration order.

The administrators remuneration is fixed either by the creditors committee or, if there is no committee, by a meeting of creditors or, failing that, by the court. If the administrator is not satisfied with the fixing of his remuneration, he may apply to the court. The administrators remuneration can be fixed either by time spent or percentage of value of assets.

The administrator is under a duty within two months after the end of each six month period after the date of his appointment to provide to the court, the registrar of Companies and the creditors committee an account of all his receipts and payments. This information must also be supplied within two months after the administrator has ceased to act.

## VAT

No formalities are required to reclaim the VAT element of the debt owed by the bankrupt-the creditor is automatically entitled to VAT bad debt relief once he has written off the debt in his books and the debt is more than 6 months old.

# GLOSSARY OF TERMS

Administrative receiver

A person appointed by the holder of a floating charge debenture over a company's assets to collect in and realise the assets of that company to repay the indebtedness to the debenture holder.

Authorised (or licensed) Insolvency practitioner

The person (usually an accountant or solicitor) authorised by the Department of Trade and Industry or a professional body to act as trustee, nominee, supervisor liquidator, administrative receiver or administrator.

Bankrupt

See undischarged bankrupt

Bankruptcy order

The court order making an individual bankrupt

Compulsory liquidation

The placing of a company into liquidation

Insolvent

A state of not being able to pay ones debts as they fall due or an excess of liabilities/assets.

Liquidation

See winding up

Liquidator

Person appointed to deal with Company in the process of being wound up

Member Shareholder
Nominee

The person chosen by an individual or corporate debtor to report on the debtors proposal for an IVA or CVA.

Official Receiver

A civil servant appointed by the DTI to head the regional offices whose responsibilities cover bankruptcy and insolvency.

| | |
|---|---|
| Proof of debt | The document submitted in an insolvency to establish a creditors claim. |
| Proxy | Authority given by a creditor or member to another person to attend and vote at a meeting on behalf of the creditor or member. |
| Receiver | A person appointed by the court for some specific purpose or the person appointed by the mortgagee to exercise his rights over the charged property. |
| The rules | The Isolvency Rules 1986. |
| Supervisor | Person appointed to supervise the implementation of the debtors proposals for an IVA or CVA. |
| Trustee | The insolvency practitioner authorised to deal with bankrupts estate. |
| Undischarged bankrupt | Person against whom a bankruptcy order has been made and who has not been discharged |
| Voluntary liquidation | The placing of the company into liquidation by resolution of the members. There are two types of voluntary liquidation: Members voluntary liquidation Creditors voluntary liquidation |
| Winding up (or liquidation) | Procedure where assets of a company or partnership are gathered in and realised the liabilities met and the surplus, if any, distributed to shareholders. |

# APPENDIX 1: COURTS DEALING WITH BANKRUPTCY

| County court | Court with bankruptcy jurisdiction | Nearest full-time court |
|---|---|---|
| Aberdare | Aberdare | Cardiff |
| Aberystwyth | Aberystwyth | Cardiff |
| Accrington | Blackburn | |
| Aldershot and Farnham | Guildford | |
| Alfreton | Derby | |
| Alnwick | Newcastle | |
| Altrincham | Manchester | |
| Amersham | Aylesbury | |
| Ammanford | Carmarthen | |
| Andover | Salisbury | |
| Ashford | Canterbury | |
| Axminster and Chard | Exeter | |
| Aylesbury | Aylesbury | Luton |
| Banbury | Banbury | Gloucester or Luton |
| Bangor | Bangor | Birkenhead or Chester |
| Bargoed | Blackwood | |
| Barnet | High Court | |
| Barnsley | Barnsley | Sheffield |
| Barnstaple | Barnstaple | Exeter |
| Barrow in Furness | Barrow in Furness | Blackpool |
| Barry | Cardiff | |
| Basingstoke | Reading | |

| County court | Court with bankruptcy jurisdiction | Nearest full-time court |
|---|---|---|
| Bath | Bath | Bristol |
| Bedford | Bedford | Luton |
| Berwick on Tweed | Newcastle | |
| Beverley | Kingston upon Hull | |
| Birkenhead | Birkenhead | |
| Birmingham | Birmingham | |
| Bishop Auckland | Durham | |
| Bishop's Stortford | Hertford | |
| Blackburn | Blackburn | Preston |
| Blackpool | Blackpool | |
| Blackwood | Blackwood | Cardiff |
| Blyth | Newcastle | |
| Bodmin | Truro | |
| Bolton | Bolton | |
| Boston | Boston | Nottingham |
| Bournemouth | Bournemouth | |
| Bow | High Court | |
| Bradford | Bradford | |
| Braintree | Chelmsford | |
| Brecknock | Merthyr Tydfil | |
| Brentford | High Court | |
| Brentwood | Southend | |
| Bridgend | Bridgend | Cardiff |
| Bridgwater | Bridgwater | Bristol |
| Bridlington | Scarborough | |
| Brighton | Brighton | |
| Bristol | Bristol | |
| Bromley | Croydon | |
| Burnley | Burnley | Bolton or Preston |
| Burton upon Trent | Burton upon Trent | Derby, Leicester or Nottingham |
| Bury | Bolton | |
| Bury St Edmunds | Bury St Edmunds | Cambridge |
| Buxton | Stockport | |
| Caernarvon | Bangor | |
| Caerphilly | Pontypridd | |
| Cambourne and Redruth | Truro | |
| Cambridge | Cambridge | |
| Canterbury | Canterbury | Croydon or High Court |
| Cardiff | Cardiff | |
| Cardigan | Carmarthen | |

| County court | Court with bankruptcy jurisdiction | Nearest full-time court |
| --- | --- | --- |
| Carlisle | Carlisle | Blackpool or Preston |
| Carmarthen | Carmarthen | Cardiff |
| Central London | Central London | |
| Chelmsford | Chelmsford | Southend or High Court |
| Cheltenham | Cheltenham | Gloucester |
| Chepstow | Newport (Gwent) | |
| Chester | Chester | Birkenhead |
| Chesterfield | Chesterfield | Sheffield |
| Chichester | Brighton | |
| Chippenham | Bath | |
| Chorley | Preston | |
| Clerkenwell | High Court | |
| Colchester and Clacton | Colchester | Southend |
| Consett | Newcastle | |
| Conwy and Colwyn | Bangor | |
| Corby | Northampton | |
| Coventry | Coventry | Birmingham |
| Crewe | Crewe | Chester or Stoke |
| Croydon | Croydon | |
| Darlington | Darlington | Teeside |
| Dartford | Medway | |
| Derby | Derby | Nottingham |
| Dewsbury | Dewsbury | Leeds |
| Doncaster | Doncaster | Sheffield |
| Dover | Canterbury | |
| Dudley | Dudley | Birmingham |
| Durham | Durham | Newcastle |
| Eastbourne | Eastbourne | Brighton |
| East Grinstead | Tunbridge Wells | |
| Edmonton | High Court | |
| Ellesmere Port | Birkenhead | |
| Epsom | Croydon | |
| Evesham | Worcester | |
| Exeter | Exeter | |
| Folkestone | Canterbury | |
| Gainsborough | Lincoln | |
| Gateshead | Newcastle | |
| Gloucester | Gloucester | |
| Goole | Wakefield | |
| Grantham | Lincoln | |
| Gravesend | Medway | |

# COURTS DEALING WITH BANKRUPTCY

| County court | Court with bankruptcy jurisdiction | Nearest full-time court |
|---|---|---|
| Grays Thurrock | Southend | |
| Great Grimsby | Great Grimsby | Hull |
| Great Malvern | Worcester | |
| Great Yarmouth | Great Yarmouth | Norwich |
| Guildford | Guildford | Croydon |
| Halifax | Halifax | Leeds |
| Harlow | Hertford | |
| Harrogate | Harrogate | Leeds |
| Hartlepool | Stockton on Tees | |
| Hastings | Hastings | Brighton |
| Haverfordwest | Haverfordwest | Cardiff |
| Haywards Heath | Brighton | |
| Hemel Hempstead | St Albans | |
| Hereford | Hereford | Gloucester |
| Hertford | Hertford | Luton |
| Hexham | Newcastle | |
| High Wycombe | Aylesbury | |
| Hitchin | Luton | |
| Holywell | Rhyl | |
| Horsham | Brighton | |
| Huddersfield | Huddersfield | Leeds |
| Huntingdon | Peterborough | |
| Ilford | Romford | |
| Ilkeston | Derby | |
| Ipswich | Ipswich | Norwich or Southend |
| Keighley | Bradford | |
| Kendal | Kendal | Blackpool or Preston |
| Kettering | Northampton | |
| Kidderminster | Kidderminster | Birmingham |
| Kings Lynn | Kings Lynn | Cambridge or Norwich |
| Kingston upon Hull | Kingston upon Hull | |
| Kingston upon Thames | Kingston upon Thames | |
| Lambeth | High Court | |
| Lampeter | Carmarthen | |
| Lancaster | Lancaster | Blackpool or Preston |
| Launceston | Plymouth | |
| Leeds | Leeds | |
| Leicester | Leicester | |
| Leigh | Wigan | |
| Lewes | Brighton | |

97

| County court | Court with bankruptcy jurisdiction | Nearest full-time court |
|---|---|---|
| Lichfield | Walsall | |
| Lincoln | Lincoln | Nottingham |
| Liverpool | Liverpool | |
| Llandrindod Wells | Welshpool and Newtown | |
| Llanelli | Swansea | |
| Llangefni | Bangor | |
| Loughborough | Leicester | |
| Lowestoft | Great Yarmouth | |
| Ludlow | Hereford | |
| Luton | Luton | |
| Macclesfield | Macclesfield | Manchester or Stoke |
| Maidstone | Maidstone | Croydon or High Court |
| Maldon | Chelmsford | |
| Malton | York | |
| Manchester | Manchester | |
| Mansfield | Nottingham | |
| Market Drayton | Shrewsbury | |
| Marylebone | High Court | |
| Matlock | Derby | |
| Mayor and City of London | High Court | |
| Medway | Medway | Croydon or High Court |
| Melton Mowbray | Leicester | |
| Merthyr Tydfil | Merthyr Tydfil | Cardiff |
| Milton Keynes | Northampton | Luton |
| Mold | Chester | |
| Monmouth | Newport (Gwent) | |
| Morpeth | Newcastle | |
| Neath and Port Talbot | Neath | Cardiff |
| Nelson | Burnley | |
| Newark | Nottingham | |
| Newbury | Newbury | Reading |
| Newcastle upon Tyne | Newcastle | |
| Newport (IOW) | Newport (IOW) | Portsmouth or Southampton |
| Newport (Gwent) | Newport (Gwent) | Cardiff |
| Newton Abbot | Torquay | |
| Northallerton | Darlington | |
| Northampton | Northampton | Luton |
| North Shields | Newcastle | |

| County court | Court with bankruptcy jurisdiction | Nearest full-time court |
|---|---|---|
| Northwich | Crewe | |
| Norwich | Norwich | |
| Nottingham | Nottingham | |
| Nuneaton | Coventry | |
| Oldham | Oldham | |
| Oswestry | Wrexham | |
| Otley | Harrogate | |
| Oxford | Oxford | Reading |
| Penrith | Carlisle | |
| Penzance | Truro | |
| Peterborough | Peterborough | Cambridge |
| Plymouth | Plymouth | |
| Pontefract | Wakefield | |
| Pontypool | Newport (Gwent) | |
| Pontypridd | Pontypridd | Cardiff |
| Poole | Bournemouth | |
| Portmadoc | Portmadoc | Birkenhead, Chester or Stoke |
| Portsmouth | Portsmouth | |
| Preston | Preston | |
| Rawtenstall | Burnley | |
| Reading | Reading | |
| Redditch | Birmingham | |
| Reigate | Croydon | |
| Rhyl | Rhyl | Birkenhead or Chester |
| Rochdale | Rochdale | Manchester or Oldham |
| Romford | Romford | |
| Rotherham | Sheffield | |
| Rugby | Coventry | |
| Runcorn | Warrington | |
| St Albans | St Albans | Luton |
| St Austell | Truro | |
| St Helens | Liverpool | |
| Salford | Salford | |
| Salisbury | Salisbury | Bournemouth or Southampton |
| Scarborough | Scarborough | Hull, Teeside or York |
| Scunthorpe | Scunthorpe | Hull or Sheffield |
| Sevenoaks | Tunbridge Wells | |
| Shaftesbury | Salisbury | |
| Sheerness | Medway | |

| County court | Court with bankruptcy jurisdiction | Nearest full-time court |
|---|---|---|
| Sheffield | Sheffield | |
| Shoreditch | High Court | |
| Shrewsbury | Shrewsbury | Stoke |
| Sittingbourne | Medway | |
| Skegness and Spilsby | Boston | |
| Skipton | Bradford | |
| Sleaford | Boston | |
| Slough | Slough | |
| Southampton | Southampton | |
| Southend | Southend | |
| Southport | Liverpool | |
| South Shields | Sunderland | |
| Spalding | Peterborough | |
| Stafford | Stafford | Stoke |
| Staines | Slough | |
| Stockport | Stockport | Manchester |
| Stockton on Tees | Stockton on Tees | Teeside |
| Stoke on Trent | Stoke on Trent | |
| Stourbridge | Stourbridge | Birmingham |
| Stratford upon Avon | Warwick | |
| Stroud | Gloucester | |
| Sudbury | Colchester | |
| Sunderland | Sunderland | Newcastle |
| Swansea | Swansea | Cardiff |
| Swindon | Swindon | Gloucester or Reading |
| Tameside | Tameside | Manchester |
| Tamworth | Birmingham | |
| Taunton | Taunton | Bristol or Exeter |
| Teeside | Teeside | |
| Telford | Shrewsbury | |
| Thanet | Canterbury | |
| Thorne | Doncaster | |
| Todmorden | Halifax | |
| Torquay | Torquay | Exeter |
| Trowbridge | Bath | |
| Truro | Truro | Plymouth |
| Tunbridge Wells | Tunbridge Wells | Croydon |
| Uxbridge | Slough | |
| Wakefield | Wakefield | Leeds |
| Walsall | Walsall | |

| County court | Court with bankruptcy jurisdiction | Nearest full-time court |
|---|---|---|
| Wandsworth | High Court | |
| Warrington | Warrington | Chester, Liverpool or Manchester |
| Warwick | Warwick | Birmingham |
| Watford | St Albans | |
| Wellingborough | Northampton | |
| Welshpool and Newtown | Welshpool and Newtown | Chester or Stoke |
| West Bromwich | West Bromwich | Birmingham |
| West London | High Court | |
| Weston super Mare | Bristol | |
| Weymouth | Weymouth | Bournemouth |
| Whitby | Scarborough | |
| Whitehaven | Workington | |
| Wigan | Wigan | Bolton, Manchester or Preston |
| Willesden | High Court | |
| Winchester | Winchester | Southampton |
| Wisbech | Kings Lynn | |
| Wolverhampton | Wolverhampton | |
| Woolwich | Croydon | |
| Worcester | Worcester | Gloucester |
| Workington | Workington | Blackpool or Preston |
| Worksop | Sheffield | |
| Worthing | Brighton | |
| Wrexham | Wrexham | Birkenhead, Chester or Stoke |
| Yeovil | Yeovil | Bristol or Exeter |
| York | York | |

# INDEX

Adjustment (of prior transactions)  70
Administration (of insolvent estates)  51
Administration  85
All liquidations  67
Application for an administration order  85
Appointing a liquidator  61

Bankruptcy (petition)  17
Bankruptcy Act 1914  7

Company Directors Disqualification Act 1986  47
Company voluntary arrangements  81
Compliance (with demand)  13
Compulsory liquidations  55
County courts  8
Creditors petitions  56
Creditors voluntary liquidations  65
Criminal action  38

Debts and dividends  71
Discharge from bankruptcy  37
Dismissal and withdrawal of petition  22
Dividends  37 73
Discharge (or variation) of administration order  88
Duties of receiver  78

Gazzette (London)  65
General control (of liquidator)  68

Hearing (the petition)  20 27 58
High court  8

Individual bankruptcy  11
Individual voluntary arrangements 8  43
Insolvency (Act)  7 43
(Rules )  11
(Partnerships)  7 47
(Proceedings Order 1986)  7
(Fees Order 1986)  7
Insolvent partnerships  47
Insolvency Practitioner Regulations 1986
Insolvent estates  51
Issue (of petition)  19
Interest  37 73
Investigation (by administrator)  89

Liquidator  60

Members voluntary liquidation 65
Mutual credit and sell off  67

Nature (of company voluntary arrangement)  83

Offences whilst bankrupt  38

Partners petition  46
Power (to deal with charged property) 87
Powers (of liquidator)  67
Powers of receiver  78
Powers of administrator  87
Priority debts in receivership  77
Provable debts  72
Public examination  61

Receivership  77
Rights of bankrupt  39

Service (of petition)  20

Statement of affairs 39-79
Statutory demand 11-54
Statutory Instrument 7
Substitution 21
Summoning (creditors meetings) 88

Trustees (and creditors) 33
Types of creditor 34

Value Added Tax. 73-79-90
Voluntary liquidations 67

Winding up (a partnership) 48

Straightforward Publishing
38 Cromwell Road
Walthamstow
London E17 9JN

For information concerning Straightforward Guides or for details of books in the series please contact Straightforward at the address above.

Alternatively, visit our web site at www.Straightforwardco.co.uk. e-mail info@straightforwardco.co.uk.